UNTUNE THE SKY

Occasional, Stammering Verse

Douglas
Wilson

Veritas
Press

First Edition 2001

Photography (except the cover photo
"Above the Clouds") and design by
Ned Bustard

ISBN 1-930710-69-0

Printed in the United States of America. We didn't want
to print this on recycled paper, but they made us.

I could not publish a volume of poetry
without dedicating it to Nancy,
who makes my life scan.

Omnes debutantae in Houstana,
carissima, non possunt
sustinere candalam tibi.

The title *Untune the Sky*
comes from a poem by John Dryden
in honor of St. Cecilia,
and refers to the final culmination
of all things in musical glory.

CONTENTS

C O N T E N T S *page 2*

Versus Profani

Poems on the Mundane

Entryway

So welcome, friend, the poems are set
And you may read them as you will
To do you good, or, yet at least
No lasting ill.

Some think that poetry should sing
And rhyme like clippings on the fridge—
To write that way of lovely things
Is sacrilege.

And others want confusing veils
So they can posture in the dark;
An ignorant revolt assails
The meadowlark.

Dear Lewis wrote of Marvell's verse,
Too free from taint, too clear for them,
That some would follow meaning's hearse
To mumble hymns.

So may I, then, from both extremes
Be safely kept away to think,
And brought through plain and pleasant dreams
To clear and subtle mountain streams,
To sweetly drink.

Motley

Come, hear ancestral Muses cry
Of wine dark sea and tumbling sky.
The king has had his blude-red wine,
Young girls lament the gurley brine.
Melodious birds sing madrigals
And music comes down waterfalls.
A man might pray with bootless cries
And sink beneath repeated tries,
As Prufrock with his trousers rolled
Will usher in an age of gold.
And poetry, which sings to scan
Will be the lot of every man.

Vineyard of En Gedi

When he gives to her, and she receives it
With passive and gentle ferocity,
He thanks his God who made their bodies fit
Within these laws of reciprocity.
So then what appears as carnal pleasure
Is really far more—it is sacrifice,
Holy and sacred, an earth-bound treasure,
Reflecting glory. I render thanks twice
For here is the woman, and here is her head
Gathered in this, their tumultuous bed.

Darkened

Oblique, opaque, and never ending,
Poets wander, ever wending
Down, still down, to the sunless sea.

A conjured image, worth the noting,
Verbs and scattered nouns are floating,
Tattered leaves upon a pond.

Profundities are in the shallows,
Water hurries in the narrows,
I wish to sit beside the fire.

And when all words astonish meaning,
Then in the fields of truth, no gleaning
Shows that poetry has died.

Deliverance

When the order finally comes
so that they roll the border under,
With the soldiers they encounter
barely meriting the name,
The chieftains of the north attack
with hard metallic thunder.
Come destroy now what is left here
of the fading Roman shame.

When the long boats come in sight of
lonely scattered coastal dwellers
And the people turn in terror
from this anger of the Lord,
Their priests and prayers are multiplied,
their maidens hide in cellars
As they see the portent coming
in an angry, bloodied sword.

We do not see what God decrees,
so then we often wonder,
Complaining much that providence
has come to be perverted.
But northern wrath, this northern rape,
this Viking greed and plunder
Is grace and mercy multiplied—
they come to be converted.

Baltimore

I walk the streets of Baltimore,
Beneath my feet, brown cobblestone.
Are these United States no more?
Her ladies weep and her patriots groan.
The blue-clad troops have lately come
To seal the Union with their force.
With measured step and angry drum,
They keep the state but kill the source
Of all confederated love,
The bond that keeps a nation whole.
Does justice see, does God above
Contend with those who seek this goal?
Beneath such questions take your stand,
And pray to God for Maryland.

Glimpse

Beneath a disappearing rain,
There amber sunlight strikes the hills,
And over green the golden stain
Spreads and so the memory fills.

The winter wheat is carpet green;
The darkening sky is battle gray;
The bright horizon in between
Is all vestigial, fading day.

The contrast of the gray and gold
(The contrast pleases more than eye)
Is nothing that our minds can hold,
Nor should we dying mortals try.

Untune the Sky

When Dryden of Cecilia spoke,
And music tumbled from his words,
It was as though all heaven broke
And fell to earth in shattered thirds.
Dumb, blind, and deaf, a beggar knows
The sweetness that can come in blows.

Ramble Tam

Ramble-tam and tumble under,
Comes the sound of marching thunder,
On the walls, defenders wonder,
Ramble-tam and tumble under.

Scramble-tam and fumble blindly,
The invader doesn't mind, he
Takes the city; thank you kindly,
Scramble-tam and fumble blindly.

Bramble-tam and stumble through it,
Tried rebellion; couldn't do it,
Long before the prophets knew it,
Bramble-tam and stumble through it.

Gamble-tam and crumble under,
Two together torn asunder,
What seemed so right was still a blunder,
Gamble-tam and crumble under.

Timber Stand

He fought with fierce and evil wolves
Before the standing timber black.
In silence he had sought their blood—
The snow would muffle any shouts.
The mechanism jammed, the metal cold,
Their murderous, bestial eyes closed round.
The rifle turned, a royal sword,
Soon wrecked their vicious hungry plans.
As one lay dead, with broken neck,
So now the others backed away.

Propriety

Everyone knows what will happen tonight,
But all politely avert the gaze,
Talking of all the beautiful sights,
The gown and veil—how the minister prays;

But later when the couple has gone
And all the trappings have been removed,
Man and woman will welcome the dawn
With eros embraced, and eros proved.

With Poles

Beside the cool and streaming waterfalls and chattering brooks
The lichen and the moss betray a trembling breeze,
While trout below still move from pool to pool
To feed on dancing sunlit bugs.
They turn and twist and leap
To lure men in
With poles
And straight lines thin,
Which no one sees them keep.
The forest floor is browning rugs
Where men, played well, will play the fool.
The lichen and the moss adorn the waiting trees,
As fish for fishermen still bait and set their lovely hooks.

Authority

The man who bends his heart and knee
Stands taller than the rest
Who dare despise authority;
For mocking fools have never guessed
Authority is submission blessed.

Knowledge

The man who sets his mind to know
And buys an ancient book,
Has gained far more than he can show
To those who with an envious look
Disdain the effort knowledge took.

Reason

The man who builds his thoughts upon
The bedrock of all thought,
Believes truth is from reason drawn—
He is the man who, praying, sought
The lesson that clear reason taught.

Love

The man who knows that God ordained
All below and all above,
Repudiates the ego stained,
Denies himself and lives in love—
The hand inside a covenant glove.

Order

The man who cultivates true peace
From chaos turns away;
He orders life and does not cease
His work to make true order stay.
He walks within an ordered way.

On Reading The Conservative Mind

I read with all the pleasure that remained,
When once I realized that Cicero
Defended Rome in just the way that Burke
Stood fast, immobile as an English oak.
The pleasure stayed, and yet I wondered how
Our institutions would receive a Christ,
Who came to bring a sword, not transient peace.
Would we recoil and say that one should die,
And then conserve our Sadducean cheat?
I am conservative; my sympathy
Lies with those men who keep their nations strong —
But may it never build a prophet's tomb.

Suburban Praise

Great God in heaven, for meat on the grill,
We glorify and praise Your name.
The sun is quiet, the grass is still,
As smoke curls through an evening tame,
From ancient times, and still the same.
We render thanks and eat our fill.

On the Advent of Silent Reading

There Ambrose, without speaking, read,
And Augustine, astounded, looked
Upon a man whose eyes could tread
The lettered page, and yet not speak.
Though mute, that reading was not blind
To oratorical display—
Eloquence within the mind!
And ancient forms lay down to die.

Gloaming

Gray ship death stands in the offing;
Listen to the ragged coughing—
And await the splash of oars.
Prostitutes bewildered, wailing,
Call for wine to help this ailing
Pimp depart for godless shores.

Hollow Years

Inside these vacant, hollow years
A man might pay for bottled tears
And lose his way in scattered fears
Before he, tumbling, falls.

A well-paid listener sagely nods
In sympathy, against all odds,
And vaguely beckons foreign gods.
Another client calls.

The incense rises, for a fee,
The truth despised will never free
The one who loves the dark won't see,
And still repentance galls.

Strider

Beneath the waves a darkened shadow glides,
As deep and swift as cold Leviathan;
The metal hull contains some deadly men,
And fluid night flows by its blackened sides.
This outer ring is where true peace resides;
The whole secure because the few have been
Assigned their watch within a watery den;
They keep the peace as strength with war collides.
At home the streets are full as men confused
About this world demand retreat from strength
And hope for something else to take its place.
But as this wish destroys the peace refused,
Those men whose minds are clear prepare at length
For war, although they would true peace embrace.

Epistemic Crisis

The terraced stages of this realm of thought
Began to trouble him beside the chattering stream
Which tumbled down, as it the green field sought.
Below the meadow fled, a dancing dream,
Below the dragonflies quicksilver seemed.
His granite thoughts, his fast compounding guilt
Began to sink in soft foundation silt.

White Falls

White falls down from the streetlight,
The sidewalk gray like a bone.
Young boy dies in a street fight;
That boy dies alone.

The Hollows

The marriage of two lonely, scattered minds
Has rarely found a wise, contented end,
And though we like to think a *choice* can free,
We still find misery the recompence.
So when these tangled hearts and minds and limbs
Have emptied meaning from the marriage bed,
Each summons accusations from the soul
And bitterly assails a mirrored self.
When randomness embraces nullity
The offspring grow, but grow without a root
Until the time arrives for *them* to take
A spouse to fill their world with emptiness.
Remember hollow souls, and tremble, true,
And speak these vows and stagger as you do.

Promises

He cannot say that all that's done is right,
He cannot think the grasping heart is true,
When men plunge into revolution's night,
And yet he still supports this bloody crew.
He sanctifies their hate with pious words,
His speech is warm; he is our Richard Price.
He tells the future from the flights of birds
And so predicts a coming paradise.
We see his love is not, and all his virtue vice.

Dark Water

Dark water settles on the rocks
And eddies wait expectantly.
The mossy boulders guard the stream
While snags cast shadows down below.
Gnats scurry in the quiet sun,
A silent watcher is undone.
Dark water settles on the rocks.

Nietzche's Limerick at Dusk

Brace for an ending of madness;
Surrender vestigial gladness.
    If you can, try to pray,
    In the embers of day,
Taste the inexorable sadness.

Experiment (1789-1865)

Those northern men who bravely fought
(and have a mighty nation wrought)
Believed they fought for liberty
And sought that right to guarantee,
While to the south their brothers knew
That noble phrases cannot do
What only virtue can. The cost?
Our great experiment was lost.

Alone

Beneath the low fire
Quiet embers waste away,
The fire gasps and dies.

Cease

Call your unkind whispering in
And silence, please, that striving tongue.
Stand, and weigh your pleasure.
Sin is old and once was young.
And faults are thick when love is thin.

The Pride of France

The pride of France is on the seas,
With Huguenots chained to their oars.
The blessed saints above invoked,
The blessed saints below decks row.

The pride of France is on the seas,
Protecting royal pimps and whores,
And murmured psalms with every stroke
Will bring this vaunted navy low.

The pride of France is on the seas,
With insolence that growls and roars.
But imprecations long-provoked,
Will take and bloody vengeance show.

VERSUS SANCTI

Poems on the Holy

Grove

How awful is this holy place
Where ash and oak and elm embrace.
The branches sway and reach and touch,
But pride defiles.

See! fallen leaves will testify
That all is grace before you lie
Beneath the sky, beneath the trees
Upon this ground.

How can a leaf itself exalt
And boast by living in the vault
Which reaches there toward the sky?
So bow your head.

To Glory

His words are white, as thunder is;
With bended neck we now are His
And will conform.

His words are dark, like distant stars.
He keeps the rain in standing jars,
And speaks the storm.

His words are bright, like pouring rain,
On new mown grass it falls again,
And blades transform.

His words bear weight, an easy yoke,
His righteousness a linen cloak,
The holy form.

Deep Red

The wine on the lees is well-refined;
This mountain is the Lord's.
A feast it is of wine on the lees;
The table is the Lord's,
A table set with all fat things,
Full of marrow, full of fat,
And wine on the lees, well-refined.

Table

The law of God is pleasant food
Which finds its way to spirit bones
So men may stand upright before
All lawless thrones.

This law of God is ordered truth
For those who under orders stand.
We cannot hate the scepter in
His gracious hand.

His enemies and ours hate law;
They agitate for legal sin.
They do not see that liberty
Is law within.

Below

Eternity and time confound
The buckling minds of mortal men,
Who rail at God as though He were
A lesser god, or one of *them.*
They hate discriminating love,
And drag it into human courts
To try to crucify the cross.
"Will you try *Me?*" our Lord retorts.
Though pearls may fall beneath the swine
They do not therefore cease to be,
And trampling won't deface a shine
Decreed before eternity.
So hold your peace, rebellious pot,
The Lord is God—and you are not.

Finally Turned

Clean moonlight fell upon the whitened grass;
The meadow filled with deep, transparent snow.
That goad again! My heart forbade me pass,
For glorious weight would surely crush below
A fearsome avalanche the idiot wretch
Who dared defile this place with noisome tread.
And so I turned away and thought to catch
My fast-escaping peace among the dead.
I went with halting step; I was constrained —
I could not leave here now; the place was still.
And so I stopped again; the moonlight reigned
Upon my sin, my poor confounded will.
I turned again, I knew not how or why.
Though I was dead, I had to pass, or die.

Evolution

Their eyes are fat like shining grease,
They hate the goodness of the law.
Where God decreed a graceful hand,
They want a filthy, mutant paw.

Invitation

Lift up the name that releases all captives,
Invite to the water all those who are drowning,
Hold out the name of the Lord Jesus Christ.
Give out the bread that can satisfy gluttons,
Offer the wine that can liberate drunkards,
Hold out the name of the Lord Jesus Christ.
Invite to the water all those who are drowning.

Breakfast

He calls to the distant and vanishing figures
And beckons them come to the fire by the shore.
Watch the fish bake as they rest on the charcoal.
This is no dead man; He offers them more.

Under a Silent Sun

We push against a silent sky
And hope to go there when we die,
But cannot see the way.

We stand upon confusing ground,
Always lost and not yet found,
And without choosing stay.

We hope, unstable, reckoning;
We don't know *what* is beckoning,
And so we wait for day.

Ungraspable

A lisping revelation creeps
Into this creaking, stupid mind.
Transcendent weighted wisdom soars;
I cannot answer this in kind.

As if a struggling beetlewit
Could name the stars, or blades of grass!
If I can ask Your favor, Lord,
Then let this crushing moment pass.

St. Paul prays we could come to know
Those glories which cannot be known
And hold in trembling, greasy hands
All that You purchased for Your own.

Your favor is no hollow thing;
You fill this universe with grace,
And so You showed Your kindness to
A sinner with a grimy face.

Elizabeth

When sons rise up to call their mother blessed
They simply say what all who know can see
That mothers fearing God surpass the rest,
And praises must be rendered thankfully.
When women leave the lot apportioned them
To grasp and grab for what is not their own
They leave behind a trail of damaged men
Whose wounds don't bleed until they've fully grown.
But those who teach, rebuke, instruct and spank
Prepare their sons to fight whom they could not
And so a grateful church has God to thank
For victories of grace by proxy fought.
And so I thank our ruling God above
For giving us a gracious present of
Elizabeth Catherine Dodds Wilson, 70 years.

Theophany at Prescott Memorial

The light streamed in the window there
and struck no heart, but one.
I heard the full crescendo where
before there had been none.
A flannel graph was facing us,
a group of three or four.
Miss Scott was busy pacing, thus,
across the wooden floor.
One figure was a paper Christ,
upon a paper cross;
He paid a handsome paper price,
and suffered paper loss.
Outside the window was a tree—
a dogwood in full bloom.
What if He suffered *there* for me,
and not inside this room?
Think if my hand had touched His side,
and not this folding chair.
What if I served the Christ who died,
and not that *thing* up there?
And if Miss Scott were Magdalene,
from seven demons freed,
Instead of one who couldn't sin,
and hadn't any need?
What if this paper lesson brought
a message—what to do?
What if from sin I had been bought,
and all this stuff is *true?*

Transition

Jerusalem left standing stones
Behind her when she fell forlorn,
But in the temple grasping groans
Relinquished faith in buried bones
And Christendom was born.

Times Square

Against it all, the preacher stands
and gives the gospel freely,
His open Bible in his hands.

His Bible's worn, his hands are too,
They've spent their years together.
All this sin is nothing new.

He lifts his voice, his voice is old,
The wind steals part away.
The people turn, their hearts are cold.

Reckoning

According to angelic census, laid
Before the bounds for nations were
Established by the One who nations made,
Those nations drew their numbered lot.

But now the ruling principalities
Behold their realms begin to shake
And try to keep the gain from such as these
Who preach with all the zeal of men.

The archon falls and from that place retreats
(the place where he received his wound),
And from that lower vantage he defeats
All those who listen to his words.

He lies — the lying does him little good
Beneath the wielded iron rod
All blinded effort vain; he never could
Withstand this nation's sovereignty.

In coming days the God of peace will crush
That ancient serpent under foot.
So then will all the frantic demons rush
Into the black, reserved pit.

Forgotten Heavens

Below the gray cathedral spire
The village lies in darkness
Which few can come to penetrate.

Below the bright celestial fire
The path of earth is markless
But leaves instead ethereal wake.

Below the highest heaven (higher
Than all the lesser dark), bless
Those who look in faith away.

Mercy Comes

Mercy comes to those who cry,
Mercy laughs and so shall I.
When this mortal life is ended,
Mercy helps the living die.

Shore to Shore

The growing kingdom fills the earth
With knowledge of the living Word;
The saints proclaim their Savior's worth;
In every tribe their voice is heard.

We do not see dominion yet;
But Jesus reigns and He will let
Us reign with Him "where e're the sun
Does his successive journeys run."

Freed Will

That I, a canon in the Mother Kirk,
Should have to go and *listen* to this man.
It is not right, it is the devil's work,
But I must hear him do what devils can.
He mounts as though the pulpit were a horse,
His text the reins, and we a gathered field.
He makes his solemn case, with building force,
And I, with fearful heart, first think to yield.
I pull it back; this man has cast a spell!
I do not *choose* to join his demons' band.
But then—effectual call!—I hear him well,
And I extend a trembling, filthy hand.
As Dagon's head lay fallen on the sill,
So tumbled down my proud, rebellious will.

Christmas Anthem

Let all the stars in the skies give praise;
Let all the heavens an anthem raise;
Come down and sing them in the shepherd's night;
Glory to God for Incarnate Light.

Let Rachel weep for her children lost,
And Ramah cry at the awful cost.
Joseph is warned in a dream to run,
And out of Egypt is called the Son.

Let Jacob's star shine in eastern skies,
And let a scepter from Israel rise;
Come down and guide the wise men to the place
Where God has visited Adam's race.

Dead Weight

When Adam weighed his lost descendants down
With grief and guilt (the ache of goodness gone),
We did not spurn his sin, but chose to drown
In waters rank with self; the weight upon
Our rebel hearts caused us to sink like rocks,
With weight that was no cold indifferent thing,
But rather trapped with living chains and locks,
So sin would bind, and living death would sting.
Now wretched men still speak of light and life
And point above the fetid water line,
But speak their words enswamped in hostile strife
Against the loving God they still malign,
Until the weight that proved the deadly loss
Is lifted, dead, down from Golgotha's cross.

A Christmas Toast

The Lollard shook his ancient, hoary head,
"I will not have your pope's tomfoolery.
A Mass for Christ?" The faithful martyr said,
"Why not a pig for Moses? You cannot see."

He died a grim and gray December day
And left behind a long-forgotten name.
Oh, may we come to learn his faith I pray,
And may we learn a faith which does the same.

And so this Christmastime I raise the glass
And bring a toast to those who hated Mass.
Their hatred was not bent—they paid the price.
I celebrate with *them* the birth of Christ.

Reformation Redux

The church is far from virtue's distant shores,
And reformation seems a pious dream.
God save us from the flattery of whores,
Whose mouths with lies like frogs in Egypt teem.
With pride their necklace, some will sail to fight
Adulterous lives and minds, adulterous legs.
With hatred sound, Ephesian men are right
But yet are given everlasting dregs.
Still others, pleasant men, are occupied
In lightly healing mortal festering sores;
They do not see their pleasant god has died,
And so they rest upon their balanced oars.
Pray love and truth unite when *God* is feared,
With Christ the only oil in Aaron's beard.

Pilgrimage

He enters in that holy place
In search of life and light, and grace.
Some candles gutter by the walls
And darkness calls.

He feels the weight; Byzantium
Is old and calmly calls to some
To serve within ancestral halls,
And darkness calls.

His spirit drawn, he turns and prays
Beneath an icon's quiet gaze;
He worships through these painted walls
And darkness falls.

Apology

The scoffer makes his sharp demand;
  He calls the faith a lie.
"Show me some proof, some argument!
  Or do you fear to try?"
But as he prates, it comes to mind
To answer folly in its kind;
  I cannot see this quarrel won
Through pointing flashlights at the sun.

Riverside

Come, all you men who hate a lie
And gather round this standard here.
All popes and bishops we defy
And tremble not, it's God we fear.

See William at the river's side
With ball in shoulder, pale, brave . . .
We still wade on to fight fat pride—
Rabble, fools, and mitred knaves.

Oh, grind these bones of ours to dust,
You still will find a marching creed,
For in predestinated trust
A man can fight and die, and bleed.

Mark the Word

Mark the word and guard your pleasure;
He whose will transcends all measure
Placed within His halls a treasure
For those of low degree.

Sacraments will feed the lowly;
Love the kind and fear the holy,
Honor God and serve Him only—
He has adopted thee.

Call for faith and in faith wonder
At this reign of silent thunder.
Apostles and the prophets plunder,
The devil's house has fallen under,
The words of Christ run free.

Stadium

Here, in death's now,
In this great concourse of saints,
We crowd together
And heaven fills.

Here, in time's gate,
In this jostling of brothers,
We look ahead
And seek light.

Here, in this tunnel,
In this press of eagerness
We strain to look
And heaven fills.

Hypocrisy

Our Savior warned of bonefilled, whited tombs
And told us how appearances deceive.
He spoke of the hypocrite, who assumes
Black can be white and wants to believe
That godly varnish can cover evil
Without cleansing and without repentance.
If given a chance to lie then he will
Deceive and place external dependance
On form, on pretence and religious show.
Gall in the wine and maggots in the bread—
So the one who thinks that God does not know
All his sin, and his rejection of the Head.
The tongue is quick, oh Lord! Hosanna save!
The face is fair; the heart an open grave.

Disgrace

Beneath a never-ending weight
of nouns eternally concealed
A man might measure years gone by,
a man could die,
Before he finally sought it out,
before his years to come
Came down upon his disappointed mind
to drive this spirit out.
So summon up the servants now—
a slavish heart revealed—
And give to all their gifts well-earned
that grace might somehow be undone.
Untold are terrifying verities,
untroubled in this blackened heart.
Is mercy really measureless?
Does mercy come to him who waits?
So grace well-earned has gathered short,
and is a grace by heaven repealed.
The fist of flesh is raised in pride;
this fire in man will kindle more
And hell below will hear the cries,
and heaven will be forever deaf
For settled was all saving grace,
and settled everlastingly
No tempests in eternity,
no traitor past those whitened gates,
No dogs within, no dangers there,
no diamonds to the man who hates.

Mystery

Immense, the mastered universe
was molded in the hands of One
Who spoke the spiraling galaxies,
and suffered them to be
A witness to His worth and strength,
His Word performing all of it.
But powers and principalities,
strong princes thronged in heavenly courts
Stood back amazed, and beckoned still,
they bowed completely down, undone
Through truth declared. This tiny world
hears truth declared by preaching men.
So God was pleased, with grace bestowed,
to give mankind fulfillment which
His prophets promised roundabout,
who preached the Word in mists and clouds.
They did not understand those depths,
dark depths a seraph cannot plumb,
But nonetheless they never ceased
to nurture staggered, simple faith
Through words that worked effectually,
through words that conquer quietly.
The Master speaks, the mastered hear
while more are called to loveliness.
So hear creation harmoniously sing
and harken to the thundering voice
Which silently suggests a prayer
and summons man's reluctant choice.

Gospel

Beneath the pressing awful weight
Of Adam's primal sin
The human race resides in hate,
And loves the death within.
With such, persuasion works in vain.
These bones will not be led.
But God takes captives in His train—
His preachers raise the dead.

Ezekiel's Threshold

The town Sychar, with Joseph's land nearby,
Contained a well which Jacob handed down.
Now once our Lord came through that place and sat
To rest because the journey had been long.
A woman came—the day was hot and dry—
To draw some water needed back in town.
The Lord requested some; she wondered that
A Jew would speak to her, for hatred strong
Had long divided her from all the Jews.
But Jesus spoke and said that if she knew
The gift of God and who had asked for drink,
She would herself have asked for what he gives—
The gift of living water she would choose.
She said, "Good sir, the well is deep, and you
Have nothing here with which to draw—I think
That you cannot excel the man who lives
Enshrined in all our memories here—the one
Who gave this well. Our father Jacob drank
From this cold spring; this patriarchal site."
Our Lord replied, "This water doesn't last,
But if you drink my gift your thirst is done.
Indeed, it will become eternal thanks
Contained within eternal life and light."
She laughed and said, "Good sir, in all my past
My thirst returns, so I return to draw.
If you will give this water, I'd be pleased."
"Go call your husband," Jesus said, "and then
Return to me—come back to Jacob's well."

"A husband? I have none," she said, but saw
Within a moment that this man had seized
Upon this point. Why did he speak of men?
"You speak the truth," he dryly said, "you tell
Me nothing but the truth. You've been through five
And now the one you have is not your own;
The words you spoke before were quite correct."
She stammered then, "Good sir, you have a gift …
The worship of our fathers still survives
Upon this mountainside where it has grown;
Jerusalem contains a place elect
By all the Jews who there their praises lift.
Which one is right? I'm sure that you can say."
The Lord declared, "The time will soon be here
When you will serve the Father neither place.
You people worship what you do not know,
While Jews have knowledge when they go to pray.
But still the time will come when childish fear
Shall be replaced and men will seek His face
In spirit and in truth. He seeks to show
Himself to worshipers who come this way,
For earthly hands cannot take hold of Him."
The woman said, "I know the Christ someday
Will answer us who live in shadows dim."
Then Jesus said, "The Christ will set you free,
And I who speak to you today am He."

Sweet Belief

Come down to the well and drink this water,
Drink the water till thirst has fled.
Thirst attends all sons and daughters,
Sons and daughters drink dust instead.
Dust pretends to pour out from a fountain,
Cisterns dry still promise relief.
Wet forgiveness from holy mountains
Flows and brings us sweet belief.

Equity

Eternity brings solemn sense
To men whose hearts are heaviness
And with the right will recompence
Within our tabernacle's tents,
That life may bless.

Word & Sacrament

The saints who gather and assemble
Come to fear the word of God.
The saints who gather come to tremble
At the triune Majesty.

The saints who gather soon are seated
At the table of the Lord.
The saints who gather well are greeted
With the bread and blood-red wine.

Wishart

Beside St. Andrews' castle wall,
Where grace was full and once bestowed,
Where sin was cruel and love was tall,
A plaque is in the road.

Father God

The swirling galaxies declare
Their Maker's praise and worth.
The heaven's proclaim Your Majesty
But we are tied to earth.

The mountains rise antiphonal
And speak from side to side.
You are the everlasting Rock,
But now our *tongues* are tied.

The thunderstorm comes from the west,
And we in silence fear.
The thunder of Your law comes down,
To tremble is to hear.

We cannot reach above our heads,
Still less Your Light proclaim
Until we learn Your grace bestowed
And pray in Jesus' name,
Amen.

Psalm First

Blessed is the man who does not walk
Where sinners stand, or mockers talk;
 The law of God is his delight,
 His meditation day and night.
By running streams his tree takes root
 And bears in season godly fruit.
Not so the wicked! their mocking laugh
 Will dissipate like wind-blown chaff.
 Under judgment, they will not stand
When fire comes down to cleanse the land.

Psalm Second

Why do the nations rage in vain?
Why do the peoples scheme?
The kings and rulers all disdain
The rule of God and dream
That they can break the hated chain
Which represents Messiah's reign.

The One enthroned in heaven roars
With laughter at the thought.
But then He turns and anger pours —
A sovereign lesson taught.
The King is crowned, all heaven adores
And sings before the palace doors.

I will proclaim the Lord's decree,
And say, "You are my Son.
I am your Father, ask from me
All lands beneath the sun.
Prepared your iron rod will be
To dash rebellious pottery."

So therefore all you kings be wise
You rulers be forewarned.
With fear submit and realize
That rebels will be scorned.
So kiss the Son, do not despise —
In Him all blessed refuge lies.

Psalm Third

Oh Lord, how many are my foes!
How many rise and dare oppose!
They laugh and mock, and then propose
That God will not deliver me.

To them, my God, I do not yield.
My Glorious One remains my shield.
To you I cry, this prayer I wield.
You answer from your holy hill.

I still lie down and go to sleep.
The Lord sustains, I do not weep.
Though enemies are thousands deep
And drawn up here on every side.

Arise, O Lord, deliver me!
With broken teeth the wicked flee.
From God, my God, comes victory
And blessing for His people here.

Psalm Fourth

Oh Lord please answer when I call!
Oh God, my strength and righteousness,
Your strength is great and mine is small —
Give me relief from my distress!

How long, oh men, will you corrupt
My glory and turn it to shame?
How long will you with lies erupt
And serve the gods who have no name?

Know that the Lord has set apart
Unto Himself all godly men.
So trembling cease! and doubt depart!
The Lord will hear my prayer, Amen!

So in your anger do not sin
When you lie down upon your bed.
Prepare your hearts and search within
Before the offered prayer is said.

While many scoff and many doubt
And say, "Who shows us any good?"
You fill us with more joy throughout
Our lives than grain or new wine could.

I will lie down and sleep in peace
For You alone, oh Lord, protect.
So let all fear and trembling cease —
The Lord will cover His elect.

Psalm Fifth

Give ear, oh Lord, to all my words
Consider all my sighs.
Please listen to this cry for help;
To you my prayers will rise.

Dawn after dawn you hear my voice.
Dawn after dawn I kneel
And lay requests before your throne
And to your strength appeal.

With you the wicked cannot dwell,
You cannot stand their ways.
Before you proud men cannot come —
On them your anger stays.

You hate those men who live in wrong.
With them your justice wars.
All lying and bloodthirsty men
The holy Lord abhors.

But I will come into your house
And seek your mercy still.
In reverence will I bow down
Toward your holy hill.

Lead me, oh Lord, in righteousness
Make straight your holy way.
My enemies are all around —
Please keep their lies away.

Declare their guilt, O sovereign God,
I cannot trust their lies.
Their throats are open tombs and graves —
Please listen to my cries.

Psalm Sixth

Oh, Lord do not rebuke me
I cannot take your wrath.
Oh, Lord please show me mercy
I faint beneath your hand.
My bones, Lord, are in agony;
I need your healing touch.
My soul abides in anguish.
How long, oh Lord, how much?

Oh, Lord turn and deliver,
Save with your steadfast love.
A dead man is no giver —
Who praises from below?
I am worn out with groaning;
I flood my bed with tears.
My eyes are weak with sorrow —
They fail in all my fears.

Depart, you evildoers!
The Lord has heard my cry.
Depart, you evildoers,
The Lord accepts my prayer.
My foes will be disheartened;
My God will shame them here.
Disgraced, they will be routed
And shall retreat in fear.

Psalm Twenty-Ninth

Give unto God, you mighty ones,
Give glory and strength!
Give all that is due to His name.
In beauty of holiness worship Him now
And let all the earth His glory acclaim.

His sovereign and majestic voice
Is over the deep;
He thunders the glorious Word.
He speaks and we hear His omnipotent call
And on all the waters glory is heard.

The cedars of all Lebanon
Break under His voice.
He splinters the forested hills.
Like yearlings they skip, and like oxen they run—
And the burning flame divides as He wills.

His voice can shake the wilderness;
The desert is filled.
His Word causes deer to give birth.
He strips forests bare; in His temple we cry
And sing "Glory!" to the Lord of the earth.

He sits enthroned above the flood;
The Lord reigns as King.
He reigns as a King evermore.
His people are strengthened with His mighty hand,
So for all His blessings let us adore.

Psalm Thirty-Fourth

I will bless the Lord at all times
And my lips will always praise.
In the Lord my soul is boasting;
Let the poor their anthems raise.
Glorify the Lord together
And exalt His name with me.
When I sought Him, how He answered!
How from fear He set me free!

Those who look to Him are radiant
And they never bow in shame.
God will save the one afflicted
When he calls upon the Name.
And the angel of the Lord will come
To encircle and protect.
Taste and see how good the Lord is —
Blessed are all our God's elect.

Fear the Lord, you saints, and worship.
Those who fear Him nothing lack.
Lions may grow weak and hungry
But the saints bring blessing back.
Come my children, come and hear me,

I will teach you — fear the Lord!
If you love your life then listen,
Listen to His holy Word.

Keep your tongue from speaking evil,
Keep your lips from telling lies.
Turn from evil, turn from danger —
Those who seek God's peace are wise.
For God's eye is on the righteous
And His ear can hear their plea.
But He turns from evildoers
To destroy their memory.

God will save the brokenhearted.
He will hear us when we cry.
Though the righteous may have trouble,
God delivers from on high.
All his bones will be protected;
Not one bone will broken be.
Though he slays all those in evil
He will set His servants free.

Psalm Fifty-Seventh

I am crying out for mercy,
God, have mercy on me here!
For my soul in You is trusting;
I will never fear.
In the shadow of Your wings,
I will take my refuge there
'Til calamities have passed me.
God, now hear my prayer.

To my God I make my groanings!
Hear my prayer, O God Most High!
You have shown to me such mercy,
O now hear my cry!
He shall send His help from Heaven,
and reproach my enemies.
God shall send forth truth and mercy;
I shall not be seized.

See my soul among the lions!
I lie down and take my rest
In the midst of those who hate me,
I still take my rest.
They are burning up with hatred,
and their words are swords and spears.
I am resting in their presence;
God saves me from fears.

Be exalted, O Jehovah!
All the heavens sing Your worth.
Let Your glory shine above us,
    far above the earth.
They have laid a net to trap me,
    they have dug it deep and long.
In the midst of their own scheming,
    they are flung headlong.

O, my heart is fixed and steadfast.
    God, my heart is set on You.
    I will praise, awake my glory,
        I will sing to You.
I will rouse the harp and lyre,
    when it seems that hope is gone.
In the dark I sing Your praises,
        I will wake the dawn.

I will praise You to the nations,
    I will sing and praise aloud
For Your mercy reaches skyward,
    truth soars to the clouds.
    Be exalted, O Jehovah,
let the heavens sing your worth.
Let Your glory shine triumphant,
    far above the earth.

Psalm Sixty-Fifth

In Zion we wait, O God hear our praise;
We shall pay our vows—no faithless delays!
Your Name shall be called "The One Who Hears Prayer."
To You all flesh come, and wait on You there.

Iniquities rise, on me they prevail.
My heart is not perfect; it commonly fails.
But as for transgressions, You always provide
And in Your perfections a sinner may hide.

But blessed is the man whom You deign to choose
And cause to approach You; He never will lose.
He dwells in Your courts and he is satisfied;
Your Temple is Holy with goodness inside.

Through terrible deeds You answer our prayer,
O God, our salvation! You answer our prayer.
The ends of the earth and the far distant seas
Are given Your signs and they fear what You please.

You rose up in strength, and founded the hills.
Your clothing is power; You do what You will.
Your Word calms the ocean; the nations of men
Are stilled from their tumult again and again.

You visit the earth, and bring in Your train
Abundance and wealth, and this wonderful rain.
The river of God flows on filled to the banks
And brings to us grain; we bring to You thanks.

Our year has been crowned with goodness and cheer;
Your paths drip abundance; it falls on us here.
The hillocks rejoice, as do cattle and grain;
They shout and they sing to the great God of rain.

Psalm One Hundred Tenth

The Lord has said to my Lord,
"My right hand is Your seat
Until I make Your enemies
Your footstool in defeat."

The Lord shall send out the rod.
All strongholds shall He seize.
The rod comes forth from Zion's hill
And rules Your enemies.

Your people have one will
In the day of Your mighty power,
Arrayed in majesty and might
Like the dew of the morning hour.

The Lord will never relent,
Through an oath His Word protects—
"You are a priest forevermore
In the line of Melchizedek."

At Your right hand is the Lord.
He shall slaughter rebellious men.
He comes to execute His wrath
On nations and kings, amen!

When our Lord's wrath is complete,
When His enemies are dead,
He will drink from a stream by the way, and then
In triumph lift His head.

The Seraph

"Now the serpent was more subtil than any beast of the field..."

Now as the great God made the heavens
And said that His making was good,
He decreed that His courtiers in sevens
Would sing what they now understood.
So the great multitude was assembled
And offered a thunderous hymn,
While the greatest of all their great number
Were the royal seraphim.

These were dragons; their wings were serrated,
And their scales all glimmered as gold.
And though they had just been created
They looked like great serpents of old.
These princes, majestic and regal,
Alone sang the thrice-holy hymn;
They flew as they sang and were splendid,
These royal seraphim.

But when the Lord God made the Garden,
And said that a man would dwell there,
The heart of one seraph was hardened,
And he fell from the sky in despair.
But still he nurtured his malice,
And his hatred was glittering, grim.
So he tempted the man and the woman,
The prince of the seraphim.

So Adam and Eve fell through sinning,
The cherubim turned them away.
But this murderer from the beginning
Still hated these children astray.
And so he vowed to pursue them
And through them to strike back at Him.
The Lord God rebuked the great dragon,
The cursed of the seraphim.

In keeping his vow he sought bloodshed
And stirred up the murderous Cain.
In the wilderness all Israel was tested,
And his brood brought them fiery pain.
They cried out to God for redemption,
Their dragon was bronzed and grim.
Nehushtan was set up before them,
The impaled of the seraphim.

Jehovah bestowed His true kindness,
And the true Son of God came down
To a race that was groping in blindness
To find the lost kingdom and crown.
God raised up the cross at Golgotha
To pillage and plunder him,
And the saints of God tread him under,
The crushed of the seraphim.

Bound Only Once

Bound only once, the Lamb of God was slain,
The hyssop red, the guilty cleansed and white.
Before the world was made the Lamb took in
    The sacrifice, and never more to die.
But minds of men this richness still disdain,
So they must bind and taunt our lesser lords,
Our gravid words which bear incarnate light,
The metaphors which speak the greater truth.
    And so they grind their syllogistic grain
To make their hollow bread, their loaves of air;
And so they tread their small Euclidian grapes
To make and drink their thin and tepid wine.
    But men will make ethereal worlds in vain,
Bound only once, the Word of God will reign.

VERSUS INCULTI

Poems on the Doggerelesque

Douglas the Mower
WITH APOLOGIES TO ANDREW MARVELL

This green and great suburban lawn
Will still be here when I am gone.
The Lord released the grass to grow;
The wife requested that I mow.
The rope pull sticks, the blades are dull,
But slow is fine; I like to mull
On days when this is all I do,
Preparing for the barbeque.

True Faith

When Darwin donned the priestly garb,
And Huxley beat the drum,
The faithful breathed the incense in
And dreamed of kingdom come—

A kingdom with millennial hope!
No God upon a throne,
No creed but chance, no law but time,
And truth? To each his own.

Saints crowded to be catechized
In holy mysteries:
How fish aspired to walk the beach;
How men came down from trees;

How whales at one time stalked the earth;
A cousin to the moose,
How science got respectable
When wisdom turned her loose.

The flock was conned, and dunned, and duped
But did not seem to mind,
For all this stuff was verified
In studies—double blind!

But here and there some sceptics spoke,
Defying all the rules
And did not seem to mind if they
Were thought to be tomfools.

They questioned what St. Charles had said,
Within his holy book,
And thought that dubious evidence
Deserved a second look.

But pious souls refused to have
This priestly work undone,
And clung to words their bishops spake —
To "just have faith, my son."

Concord Jelly

By the rude man who arched his brow,
His wit to April's breeze unfurled,
Here stood the farmer by his cow
And fired the quip heard round the world.

Spring

The birds are roaring in the trees;
And fish are clanking through the seas,
White clouds still rattle by.

The mild breeze is thundering
And zephyrs stomp through, blundering
Into my eager eye.

The green buds ope explosively;
This poet could get close if he
Would only try
Harder.

The Way It Goes

Pecunia saepe volabit,
Semper stultus vocabit.
"Fortuna, mane!
Fortuna, vide!"
Tamen Fortuna non audit.

True Philosophy

A poem is a thought
That always sounds good,
And lingers a while
But it doesn't have to rhyme
(though it could).

Making Sense

Doggerel is as doggerel does,
Words spin around like tumble-dried clouds,
Comic verse, frankly, just ain't what it was
And suffers beneath all these shimmering shrouds
For doggerel is as doggerel does.

Doggerel is as doggerel knows,
Words rattle round like knives in the dryer.
Humility looks to the muse who bestows—
A poet who's bashful is just that much shyer
For doggerel is as doggerel knows.

Doggerel is as doggerel trumpets,
Words blat their way like claxons and horns
At the great banquet throw bread rolls and crumpets
And howl like a band of sore Saxons in thorns
For doggerel is as doggerel trumpets.

Doggerel is as doggerel oozes,
Where is your Virgil, your Homer, your Horace?
Where is your master, the laureate snoozes
While all this great while we rhyme in a morass—
For doggerel is as doggerel oozes.

Trouble

Tonight the words don't seem to come
Tonight the meter doesn't fit
And still I write, and still believe
Ut hic poeta docebit.

Tonight the muse is late again
Tonight the muse has not carressed
These lines which wait, impatiently,
Enim "Carmen bonum est."

Tonight I think to give it up
Tonight I shall lay down the pen.
It does no good, I think, to make
An ancient muse American.

Wimp's Lament

The blues come back to haunt me now
When I recall you've gone away;
I've lost you to another—how?
I said "I love you" every day;
I gave you hugs, and flowers too.
I nurtured our relationship;
I fixed you quiche and cordon bleu,
But all you gave was lots of lip.
You said, "I want a real man
Who doesn't put up with my racket
When I say I want him to pack it."
I need a new plan;
I must be a man
And learn to be tough and hack it.

Dubito Ergo Sum

When I doubt I have to be doubting,
And in order to doubt I must be;
This is more than sophistical flouting
Of the Cartesian in me.

Opinions

I loathe, I hate,
Abominate
White, vinyl fences.
I hate, despise
All slipshod lies,
Viz. wine in boxes.
I chafe, I spit,
I writhe a bit
When listening to music by Andrew Lloyd-Weber.
And if I can
Return to scan
I'll close with caution.
Thank you very much.

Baffled

Tall he was and rugged bellus
David pulcher fuit.
Got a secret he won't tell us
But still the ladies knew it.

Celebratory Doggerel

The lima bean
Said, "I'm a bean,
And I don't care you know it."

The yellow squash
Said, "Pish and posh,
So I suggest you stow it."

Watermelon,
Convicted felon,
Said, "If it's too big, then tow it."

The green bean pole
Said, "I've got no soul! . . .
My static state doth show it."

The green grass round
The garden found
That poets tend to blow it.

The poet grim
Said, "*I'm* not him.
When grass is thick, you mow it."

Disappointment

Cumulo-bumpus clouds threaten the picnic,
Spirits are sodden and happiness sags.
Watch as the green grass bestirs in a panic
And rain starts to smack our potato chip bag.

Ode to the Bish

There once was a bishop named Spong
Who decided to just get along.
He embraced the *zeitgeist;*
In a churchified heist,
And sold out the Creed for a song.

Subtle Glory

Her laughter scuttles like a crab
And settles down beneath some rocks.
Her hands are chapped; her linen drab,
She pushes back dishwater locks.
And yet each day as it occurs
Amusement stirs.

The Night Before Whatsit

'Twas the night before Christmas and all through the land,
We still mark the birth of the One who is banned
From public discussion or public display.
"Get rid of the Christ child—but still keep the day!"
So public school children must practice with stealth
Those carols which threaten our strange commonwealth,
And now and again someone's runaway creche
Will abruptly appear in some government place,
Right out in the open where *children* can view
This threat to the folks at the ACLU.
So drink to the health of our once happy nation,
And deck all the halls with strange litigation.
Then eat all you want to, drink rum by the quart
But don't say that name, or you'll wind up in court.
Pretend that this holiday just always was.
Don't ask whence it came like a smart child does.
Just talk about Rudolph or Santa's small elves,
Or sing little ditties of days bunched in twelves.

Now this is all right because (please get this straight)
There's no separation of North Pole and state.
So sing all you want of this sort of stuff
In the public arena, folks can't get enough.
If you do sing the carols, then please, just be careful.
Look over your shoulder, keep watch and be prayerful.
Edit those carols, avoid our law's curses,
(You'll have to leave out quite a few of the verses.)
So you won't get the secular humanists riled
With songs about sinners and God reconciled.
"Be near me Lord Jesus, I ask Thee to stay,"
Angers the People for the Humanist Way.
But if you believe the time is now ripe
To stand up for Christmas, don't sit there and gripe.
The secular Scrooges and Grinches will hear
If you say, "Merry Christmas," with all the right cheer.
It's time to be counted for what's good and right,
To all, Merry Christmas! To all, a good night!